Stepping Back into the Light

Leigh Bamford

Presentation by *BookLeaf Publishing*

Web: www.bookleafpub.com

E-mail: info@bookleafpub.com

ISBN : 9789357447751

First edition 2021

DEDICATION

I dedicate this book to all who have struggled with fear and despair, but kept going regardless, and also to the frontline NHS staff and care workers, whose dedication to their job was inspirational to me.

ACKNOWLEDGEMENT

I would like to acknowledge many people. My family and friends for supporting my writing work, knowing, as they do, how much it means to me. My teachers at Alderman Davies CIW Primary School, Ysgol Hendrefelin, and my lecturers and support workers at NPTC and UWTSD. They supported my passion for writing and I wouldn't have written this without that support. I would also like to acknowledge BookLeaf Publishing itself for offering this opportunity to me.

PREFACE

You are not alone, it hasn't just happened to you, it has happened to everyone on the planet, so we are in this together. As humans, it is our duty to help each other through difficult times, and this is my way of helping those reading this right now. Throughout lockdown I have been working on building my faith and my optimism: They were my best weapons for battling embitterment. Here you will find a collection of poems that will hopefully help you do the same.

Swarming

Days come to be sunny, yet emotion sticks to you, like your own shadow. Many fight it to keep the sun in their hearts, but you are not wrong if you wish to let the weight swarm about you for that moment of the day. One of the best choices is to let it flow like a cold. Like a cold, sadness is temporary.

Someone

It's not just something that can interfere with one's deserving happiness of life, but 'someone'. Sometimes someone can be of many someones that make you feel insecure, unsure and desperate to hide. There is no right or wrong to hide or confront. Speak your mind if you feel strong enough, but hiding is unconditional if one wishes to be safe. Certain someones may leave an impact, but you will carry on with the day feeling something about yourself. An individual someone who is happy to be that someone, and not be the someone whom had upset you. Get ready to be the bright someone that the world wants and deserves.

Witnessed Eyes

Very often in October, in my witnessed eyes, it rains heavily. Furthermore it is coming on very cold. Despite the discomfort, the sun appears every now and then. When it does, enjoy while it's there for the rain may return, but then many might not want to raise their own hopes then and there. But on the other hand, I can hardly wait for a cold autumn day, sunny for hours on end. What about you?

The Voice

Loneliness is nobody's thing. But if one thinks deep, back then there was no electricity or keyboards; just paper and pencils. With the two formers, you don't need pencils or papers. Yes, words are immortal once printed, but the sheer beauty of hearing the voice. The voice is an instrument to isolation thanks to the internet. Do not despair much longer because loneliness is forgotten when the voice comes into earshot.

Then and Now

Frequently, often if anything, I reflect upon then. Then seems the more brighter chapter of my life as I sit or stand in the middle of these current years, years of misery, depression, loss and anything negative. But now is the time to make a bright then to go with your previous then. Memories are precious, but reflect upon then as you recall your positive feelings and use it in the time of now. We're all standing and sitting and writing and reading. Get started, now.

The Feel

Loss is something we all have in common in families. My life is no longer the life I am used to, yet I find myself facing issues without backing away, though I want to. I am asking those whom I have lost, are you aiding me through the struggles you yourselves had probably encountered? It must be, for I never dared myself to confront or take risks. I see and hear none of them, but I clearly feel them. Can you feel whom you have lost? I'm still scared, but with the feel of them within me, and you, we are all strong together and can push ourselves out of the darkness.

Chocolate Milk

When in such a dark predicament, positivity seems to drain from you like a carton of chocolate milkshake. With the carton drained, what are you left with? The memory of taste, but you will have another top up soon. With positivity drained from your emotions, what are you left with? Hope. Positivity can be a memory, but hope is never a memory to begin with, since everyone finds it somewhere inside themselves. Hopelessness is an existing feeling, but hope is like an empty carton of chocolate milk; refilled to savour the flavour and ready to relive.

Only Clouds

Rain comes the most often in this world, so it seems. But then there are days where we have no rain, but no sun either. Only clouds are visible to the human eye, but with there being no rain, there is a chance for you to venture outside before it may eventually start, and muster your strength to walk, despite the dark sky. Rain or shine, the chance is there and you can have it.

Food for Thought and Taste

Even when down, something laughable may not work, so what can we do? Eat. Why eat? Go to a restaurant and when your buds react, the flavour shall make you beam. Flavour makes us happy, and if happy from a flavour, happiness is obviously right by your side.

The iPod

I recall a time, one cold night, I reflected on everything going on; masks concealing everyone's lovely smiles and hugs being forbidden, due to the thief of joy. I reflected on it all and I cried. But I remedied it. Not with medicine, not with pills, not with happy thoughts, but with the iPod. My saviour of depression, for a library of hopeful melodies and voices reside in the box. When sad and tearful, switch on the music and surround yourself with the beauty it brings to your ears. Listen until the dawn breaks.

In Bed

We find ourselves in no place but bed when a new day is born. Somewhere cozy, somewhere warm, somewhere protective. But to rely on your cot will prevent you from living. Rise and shine, step outside your house, travel and try to be someone who can right a wrong world - even to find something worth your life.

Me Too

Ever have days of gloom? Me too. Just because I write poems of optimism doesn't mean I'm incapable of negative thoughts. It's in everyone we know who smiles everyday, me too. But to assure ourselves, the rain will calm down and we will be rewarded with the sun - followed by a rainbow.

Pitch Dark of Night

Night is the scariest time of the clock to tick up to. Even when you sleep in one room, fear comes into your head and noises outside a room joining in. But humans are sensible, therefore we must be firm and say "It's the brain!". Soldier through the night, for dawn is only hours away - and for you to catch up on some sleep if needed. Soldiers deserve a break.

The B Word

When met with anything that interferes with our wellbeing, we are almost immediately greeted with the first sentence in our mind: "I will never make it". Savour the idea that your mind said it, not you. Only you can talk and not the mind. So the one solution is to say out loud, the B word; BELIEVE! Whisper it, say it, shout it, scream it. What happened to us these past two years were a burden, but you obviously believed you could find your way out despite the rainclouds that rained on you - and me. Finishing this sentence, say the B word to yourself, and here is where the sentence ends.

It's Coming

There are times we walk, there are times we run, there are times we climb. Sadness is like a mountain we climb; it's a burden and we cannot bring ourselves to reach the top, but we can keep climbing by force because above is the end of everything, that started the fears in this world that started last year. It may take time, but it's coming.

Good Morning

Good morning. Did you sleep well? Good if you did, if not, well never mind. It's morning now. Whether your dreams were pleasant or vile, there's always a morning to wake up to. It's nice to wake up to sunshine, but if it rains then bring yourself to smile anyway, because I'm always happy to wake up to a new morning at all. Next plan is to make the day a memorable one.

Adventures of the New

Where tree leaves fall, tree leaves grow. Where negativity flows, positivity blooms. What do these things have in common? New. Things change in our lives eventually, but then the new is expecting us. Simply go for a walk, ride your bike or drive your car. You will see that there are the same things in eyesight, but any minute now, a new is coming your way and with any luck, it's a new you will love.

Within the Books

Trapped in a world of strife, there are other places to visit and they are located within the pages of books. Open your page and you are fighting for justice, venturing the unknown, discovering your inner-self and meeting they who will help you see the light and emerge a warrior. Look within the books, like you are doing right now.

Dream

A feeling inside us; it's not very pleasant and it's not very sweet. Emotion is what we all have in common. But give it time and let it bother you, for it cannot do so forever. But to get rid of it early, solider on and carry on with what God put you on this planet for; talent and interest. As you display your talent and interest, the emotion weakens due to it. Go to sleep elated, for horrid emotions and feelings, are only a dream.

Can and Will

As the weather grows cold, we are reminded of the cold times that we remember. But reading my words, I live in hope that I helped many discover the strength they hold within. You can do it, emerging from the dark and restoring your lives. Can and will. For everyone deep down has the will.

Five Words

Love, faith, connection, courage and strength. Five words that we brought with us through this journey. Something proven by the actions of people I see, hugging, gaining the confidence of losing their masks and forgetting about sanitising and resuming their jobs. With those five words, you can assure yourself that things are coming back to normal. With that in mind, the five words and all, the world 'will' come back to normal. It won't be long now.

www.ingramcontent.com/pod-product-compliance
Lightning Source LLC
La Vergne TN
LVHW050505210726

843509LV00015BA/3002